What Was the Lewis and Clark Expedition?

by Judith St. George

illustrated by Tim Foley

Penguin Workshop

To Chance. Happy traveling wherever you go,
with love and best wishes from your
grandmother Judith—JSG

PENGUIN WORKSHOP
An Imprint of Penguin Random House LLC, New York

Text copyright © 2014 by Judith St. George.
Illustrations copyright © 2014 by Penguin Random House LLC. All rights reserved.
Published by Penguin Workshop, an imprint of Penguin Random House LLC, New York.
PENGUIN and PENGUIN WORKSHOP are trademarks of Penguin Books Ltd.
WHO HQ & Design is a registered trademark of Penguin Random House LLC.
Printed in the USA.

Library of Congress Control Number: 2014028649

ISBN 9780448479019   20 19 18 17 16 15

Contents

What Was the Lewis and Clark Expedition? . . . 1

The Cocaptains 6

The Journey Begins 12

Winter Sets In 24

Sacagawea 31

Pushing Off 34

Travel on the Rivers 40

A Homecoming 50

In and Out of Fort Clatsop 70

The Return Trip 77

Setbacks 89

Arriving Home 96

Timelines 106

Bibliography 108

What Was the Lewis and Clark Expedition?

In history books the names of two men, Meriwether Lewis and William Clark, are always linked. Their names could almost be one word: LewisandClark. They had much in common. They were both from Virginia. Both served in the US Army in the late 1700s, where they became friends. Both men were intelligent and brave. Born leaders, they were experienced woodsmen who could survive in the wild. But their names are linked because together they were cocaptains of a famous journey across the North American wilderness. They headed up a two-year-long trip all the way from the Midwest to the Pacific Ocean—and back again. Their journey became known as the Lewis and Clark Expedition.

In 1801, when Thomas Jefferson became

the third president, the country was made up of seventeen states. The country went only as far west as the Mississippi River. In 1803 the United States paid France fifteen million dollars for a huge parcel of western land—828,000 square miles. The sale, which was called the Louisiana Purchase, more than doubled the size of the United States! In time, many states would be carved out of the land—Arkansas, Missouri, Iowa, Oklahoma, Kansas, Nebraska—as well as parts of other states—Minnesota, North Dakota, South Dakota, Montana, Wyoming, Colorado, New Mexico, Louisiana.

President Jefferson believed that the future of America lay in the West. Now that so much new land belonged to the United States, he wanted to have it explored. He hoped to find a waterway across North America to the Pacific Ocean. He wanted to learn all about the western Indian tribes and their way of life. Controlling the rich western fur trade was another of Jefferson's goals.

So what did Jefferson do? He planned for a party of explorers to take a river trip across North America. Nobody knew what they would find.

Thomas Jefferson

Thomas Jefferson was born April 13, 1743, in Shadwell, Virginia. At twenty-six, after his father died, he inherited a large estate and built a house called Monticello on it. Jefferson, who owned some two hundred slaves, lived at Monticello for most of his life, except for the years he spent in Paris and his eight years in the White House. At twenty-eight, he

married Martha Wayles Skelton. They lived happily together until her death ten years later. Although Martha had given birth to six children, only two daughters lived to adulthood.

As a member of the Second Continental Congress, Jefferson wrote a document that is revered and respected to this day—the Declaration of Independence. After the thirteen colonies became the United States of America, Jefferson served as secretary of state under his Virginia neighbor, America's first president, George Washington. In 1796, he became vice president under the second president, his old friend John Adams. Four years later he was elected as the third president of the United States, serving two terms, from 1801 to 1809. One of his foremost achievements was the Louisiana Purchase. Thomas Jefferson died on the same day as John Adams. That day was July 4, 1826, the fiftieth anniversary of the signing of the Declaration of Independence.

CHAPTER 1
The Cocaptains

President Jefferson didn't waste any time organizing the trip west. In 1803, he chose his secretary, Meriwether Lewis, to command what was called the Journey of Discovery. The explorers going with Lewis would be called the Corps of Discovery. Lewis asked a good friend from his army days, William Clark, to be his cocommander. Clark's reply was an enthusiastic yes.

The two men's personalities were very different. Lewis was better educated. He tended to be moody, thoughtful, and a worrier. Lewis was not a scientist, but he prepared for the trip by reading many of the books in Thomas Jefferson's library. Jefferson had Lewis study mathematics, surveying, mapmaking, fossils, anatomy, natural history, astronomy, botany, medicine, and anything else that would be helpful on the journey.

The redheaded Clark was more a man of action. He had a temper, but he was also friendly, likable, optimistic, and practical. In almost every encounter, he got along well with the Native Americans. When the Indians needed medical attention or wanted advice, they would almost always ask for the "redheaded one."

Meriwether Lewis

Meriwether Lewis was born in Albemarle County, Virginia. The Lewises and the Jeffersons were good friends. Jefferson knew Meriwether from the time of Meriwether's birth on August 18, 1774.

After serving in the Army, Lewis became President Thomas Jefferson's secretary. He was honored when the president picked him to lead the Corps of Discovery. Lewis always said the highlight of his life was his trip through the wild Northwest.

In October 1809, on his way to Washington, Lewis stopped at an inn in Natchez, Tennessee. He was found, shot dead, the next morning. It is not known whether he had committed suicide or was murdered.

William Clark

William Clark was born on August 1, 1770, in central Virginia. However, the Clarks soon moved to Louisville, Kentucky. William, who enlisted in the Army in 1789, joined a regiment to protect Kentucky settlements from Indian attacks.

In 1803, when the offer from Lewis came to colead the expedition, Clark replied: "My friend, I join you with hand and heart." The government awarded Clark 1,600 acres and $1,228 in back pay for his two years service with the Corps of Discovery. He was named governor of the Missouri Territory in 1813.

After his second wife died in 1831, William Clark moved to St. Louis to live with his eldest son, Meriwether Lewis Clark. He died there on September 1, 1838.

The two captains' different personalities made for a perfect balance. Despite danger, hunger, and other hardships, the two men worked side by side. No one in the Corps ever heard a serious argument between them. With two such capable captains, it wasn't hard to recruit army men to join the Corps. Twenty-three US Army privates and three US Army sergeants signed up. York, Clark's African American slave, came along, too. So did Lewis's Newfoundland dog, Seaman.

Jefferson told the two captains it was important to keep careful records and make maps of their travels. The cocaptains were to send back reports and samples of their discoveries. They were to write in their journals every day, describing what they saw and found—animals, plants, and minerals "not known in the United States."

Lewis and Clark had no idea what they would encounter. There were stories of a huge mountain range—the Rocky Mountains. Would they find it? And would they return home to tell about it?

CHAPTER 2
The Journey Begins

Jefferson wanted the expedition to start as soon as possible. Because most of the Journey of Discovery would be by water, a fifty-five-foot barge was built for the explorers. Known as a keelboat, it had sails and twenty oars—ten on

keelboat

ogue

each side. Not only would it carry men, food, and supplies, but it would also carry gifts for trading with the Indians they encountered along the way. Canoes and two pirogues would also carry men and supplies. Pirogues were large rowboats with sails. One pirogue had a red sail, the other a white sail.

The expedition was first based opposite the settlement of St. Louis, where the Mississippi and the Missouri Rivers met. The men would wait out the winter there.

By the spring of 1804, everyone was eager to get started, including Lewis. But first, he had to leave camp to buy supplies and food. The men had to take everything they needed except for

meat that they would hunt and fish that they would catch in the wilderness.

Because there were no maps to follow, Lewis bought surveying equipment—a compass, a quadrant, and a sextant. He also bought clothes for each man—an overcoat, a raincoat, overalls, shirts, and socks. However, Lewis knew that in the wilderness new clothes would wear out quickly. When they did, the men would have to make clothing from animal skins, and the way to get skins was to hunt local wild animals. So he purchased guns and ammunition. Weapons were also needed in case they had to fight off hostile tribes, although Jefferson ordered the explorers to do everything possible to stay on friendly terms with the Native Americans.

Lewis decided that the Corps should take the standard military amount of liquor, and almost 200 pounds of dried, condensed soup, called "portable soup," which could be used in an emergency. As for other food, Lewis made sure that the corps had 3,400 pounds of flour, 560 pounds of biscuits, and 750 pounds of salt, as well as coffee, peas, beans, sugar, lard, and candles. Lewis noted in his journal that he bought pots, axes, drills, files, and other "Tools of every Description." He also made sure to pack hundreds of pounds of goods to trade with the Indians they met along the way—colored glass beads, ribbons, needles, knives, fishhooks, calico shirts, scissors, copper kettles, blankets, tobacco, ear and nose trinkets, and dozens of other items that would appeal to the Indians. On the advice of a well-known Philadelphia doctor, Lewis also packed medicines.

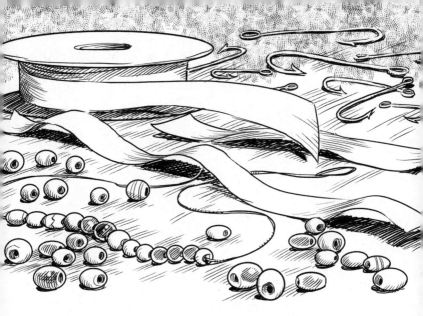

Last but not least, Lewis ordered a forty-foot-long boat be constructed, mostly of iron. The forty-four-pound frame could be carried overland. Later on, it would be covered with hides or bark. Lewis wrote about the iron boat with great pride: "It is much stronger . . . will carry its burthen [burden] with equal ease, and greater security; and when the bark and wood are discarded, will be much lighter, and can be transported with more safety and ease."

Congress had granted the expedition $2,500 for their supplies and food. Lewis bought everything they needed for a little more than $2,000. Even though Lewis hadn't finished shopping, Clark started out. Clark and the Corps packed up and pushed off with great excitement. Lewis wrote in his journal what Clark had told him of their leave-taking. Local citizens came to cheer them off with shouts of good luck and safe journey: "at 4 P.M. on Monday the 14th of May 1804, he [Clark] embarked with the party in the presence of a number of the neighbouring Citizens who had assembled to witness his departure."

No doubt each man had his own fears. What Indians would they meet? Would they be hostile or friendly? What dangerous animals would there be? Would they find enough game to kill and eat for survival? How long would it be before they saw their families again?

Clark and his crew headed west into the mouth of the Missouri River. A week later, Lewis, with all his purchases, caught up to them.

The Corps soon found out that traveling on the river wasn't easy. Sandbars, snags, and rapids slowed them down. Floating logs were a danger. A big log hitting a pirogue or canoe could crush it. Sometimes the team traveled only a mile an hour.

Rain, rain, and more rain, intense heat, and clouds of mosquitoes made everyone miserable, even Lewis's dog, Seaman. Lewis and Clark complained often in their journals about the swarms of mosquitoes:

"The mosquitoes and ticks are noumerous & bad."

"The musquitoes are yet troublesome."

"The musquetoes continue to infest us in such manner that we can scarcely exist . . ."

". . . my dog even howls with the torture he experiences from them . . ."

". . . they are so numerous that we frequently get them in our throats as we breath."

There were times of fun and fellowship, too. On August 18, the boats were tied up on the Missouri River's banks for Meriwether Lewis's thirtieth birthday. The men square-danced late into the night. Clark wrote: "Cap L. Birth day the evening was closed with an extra gill of whiskey and a Dance until 11 oClock."

One sergeant missed the festivities. "Serjeant Floyd is taken verry bad," Clark wrote in his journal. "He gets wordse [worse] and we are muc allarmed at his Situation."

Floyd had a burst appendix. Without proper medical care, Floyd died on August 20, 1804, and was buried on a hilltop overlooking the Missouri River that the explorers named Floyds Bluff. Charles Floyd was the only person on the expedition to lose his life.

CHAPTER 3
Winter Sets In

A death so soon after their trip began must have been worrisome to Lewis and Clark, but they had no choice but to keep traveling north on the river. From late July to early November they met up with many Indian tribes, most of whom were friendly. Lewis and Clark joined the Indians in smoking peace pipes. They also gave the chiefs Jefferson medals. The Indians especially treasured blue glass beads. Clark's slave, York, fascinated the Indians. Thinking his dark African American skin was paint, they tried to rub it off.

Of all the tribes they met, the Teton Sioux were the most hostile. However, even the Teton Sioux were willing to sit down with Lewis and Clark. In the end, the Teton Sioux allowed the Corps to continue on.

Winter arrived. By late November 1804, they had traveled 1,600 miles from St. Louis. There were still 1,000 miles to go to reach the Pacific Ocean. Snow was falling, and the Missouri River was freezing over. It was time for the explorers to build their winter quarters. All the men pitched in to build a fort on the Missouri River's banks near several villages where 4,400 Indians made their home.

The fort went up quickly. It had two rows of log huts, a storage shed, a smokehouse, and

a sentry box. An eighteen-foot-high stockade fence made of sharp-pointed logs surrounded the buildings. "We called it Fort Mandan, in honour of our friendly neighbours," Lewis wrote.

Their friendly neighbors included not only the Mandan tribe but also the Minnetarees. The natives visited the fort and welcomed the Corps members into their earth lodges. The lodges were large, round, domed buildings built of sod.

Lewis and Clark wrote to Jefferson describing the natives' way of life.

The winter of 1804–1805 was bitterly cold. The temperature sometimes dropped to almost forty degrees below zero. Herds of buffalo walked on the frozen Missouri River without breaking through the ice.

On Christmas and New Year's Day, most of the men were homesick. They received no mail or gifts from their families back home. Nevertheless, they exchanged presents and enjoyed food, drink, and square dancing.

That winter, two more people joined the Corps. A fur trader named Toussaint Charbonneau and his young Native American wife appeared one day. Charbonneau knew sign language and many Indian languages. Lewis and Clark persuaded him to travel with the Corps. Charbonneau would act as their translator. His wife could come, too. Her name was Sacagawea.

Sacagawea, who was going to have a baby, was a member of the Shoshone tribe. The Shoshones were famous for their herds of horses. Lewis and Clark had been told that the Corps would need horses to cross the Shining (Rocky) Mountains. But Charbonneau didn't speak the Shoshone language. Later on the Corps' leaders would have to depend on Sacagawea to barter with the Shoshones for the horses they would need.

CHAPTER 4
Sacagawea

On February 11, 1805, Sacagawea gave birth to a fine, healthy boy. His father named him Jean Baptiste, but Clark came up with the name Pompy, meaning "little chief" in the Shoshone language. Soon everyone called him Pompy or Pomp. Having a baby around was a happy reminder of home and family to all the men.

Like the explorers, Sacagawea was far from home, too. A Minnetaree war party had captured her when she was just a young girl picking berries with other Shoshone women and children.

For five years Sacagawea lived as a Minnetaree slave on the Missouri River, hundreds of miles from home. The Minnetarees named her Sacagawea. *Sacagawea* meant "Bird Woman." When she was sixteen, Toussaint Charbonneau, who was more than twenty years older, took her for his wife. When Sacagawea married, she was no longer considered to be a Minnetaree slave. However, her husband didn't speak Shoshone, and Sacagawea didn't speak French. They spoke to each other in Minnetaree, which they both knew. They met up with the Corps about a year after their marriage.

When Sacagawea learned that Lewis and Clark wanted horses from the Shoshones, she was thrilled. That meant she would be going home. Home!

At last spring arrived. Plans were made for pushing off. For her first long journey, Sacagawea wore her best clothing: deerskin leggings, moccasins, a fringed garment decorated with elk teeth, and a blue-beaded belt. She also wore bracelets, earrings, and finger rings. She planned to wear all these handsome clothes again when they reached the land of the Shoshones. She would be seeing her family and old friends after all this time.

CHAPTER 5
Pushing Off

On April 7, 1805, seven soldiers, five boatmen, and an Indian guide headed back down the Missouri River in the keelboat. They were to deliver cargo to President Jefferson and his scientists. This would be the first news that Jefferson received from the expedition. On board were reports, letters, maps, charts, rocks, plants, fur robes, Indian tools and weapons, animal skeletons, antlers, and horns. A live prairie dog

and magpie were also making the trip. No one back east would have ever seen a prairie dog or a magpie.

On that same day, thirty-three members of the Corps boarded the red pirogue and six dugout canoes that had been hollowed out over the winter. Sacagawea, with Pomp, her husband, and a few other men, rode in the white pirogue. The Corps left Fort Mandan and headed west on the Missouri River.

One day, a squall blew up, and the white pirogue heeled over. Sacagawea quickly snatched Pomp from his cradle bundle and handed him to her husband. She knew what she had to do next. Papers, letters, journals, a medicine kit, and instruments had fallen into the water. Luckily, they had all been packed in watertight bags.

Sacagawea knew the bags were important to Lewis and Clark. She grabbed whatever she could reach that came floating by. In the end, everything was saved. It was one of the many times Sacagawea proved her importance to the Corps. Lewis praised Sacagawea for her bravery and cool head.

Grizzly Bears

Grizzly bears presented another danger. They were a new and fearsome enemy. A full-grown male grizzly bear could weigh as much as one thousand pounds. When standing on his hind feet he was more than six feet tall. Some bear tracks were almost a foot

long. These reddish-brown bears were nothing like the bears that the Corps members had encountered back east. Because of their silver-tipped hair, the Indians called them white bears. When Indians hunted grizzlies, they dressed and painted for war.

Once a terrified Corps member shot and wounded a grizzly that chased him for half a mile. Luckily, the soldier was saved when Lewis killed the bear with a shot to his head. Only a bullet to the head or heart would kill a grizzly.

Another time, six soldiers saw a full-grown male grizzly. When two of their shots hit the bear's lungs, he charged. Two more shots struck the wounded bear. Still, he kept coming. Two of the soldiers jumped in the river to escape the bear's fury. But the bear jumped in and swam after them. He had almost reached the two men when a man on shore shot and finally killed him.

In his journal, Lewis summed up his thoughts: "I . . . had reather fight 2 Indians than one bear."

CHAPTER 6
Travel on the Rivers

Always keeping a sharp eye out for grizzlies, the Corps kept heading west until they arrived at the place where the Yellowstone and Missouri Rivers met. The explorers knew that the Yellowstone River would lead them to the Columbia River and from there to the Pacific Ocean. It was an important milestone. To celebrate, one of the men

played his fiddle and the soldiers square-danced. Lewis and Clark gave each man whiskey.

Five weeks later, the Corps came to another fork in the river. This time they were not sure which way to go. The wrong fork would lead them into deeper wilderness. The correct fork would meet up with the Yellowstone River.

Lewis and Clark explored both forks while the soldiers rested. The men needed a break. Game was scarce and everyone was hungry. Most of the men were sick with colds, fevers, and boils. It had rained for days. Mosquitoes tortured them. The thorns of the prickly pear cactus had cut the men's feet right through their moccasins.

After five days of exploring, Lewis and Clark decided that the explorers should take the south fork. It was the right choice. The Corps hid their red pirogue, then buried dried food, supplies, and gunpowder in a pit called a cache. They would pick up everything on their return trip.

On June 10, 1805, Lewis and four other men went on ahead to the Great Falls. From seven miles away they could hear the falls' thunderous roar. The Missouri River tumbled down one waterfall after another for a stretch of five waterfalls. Some falls dropped as much as six hundred feet. Lewis wrote in his journal that the Great Falls were "the grandest sight I ever beheld."

Six days later, Clark and the other Corps

members caught up with Lewis at the Great Falls. They hid the white pirogue, and buried what they wouldn't need until their return trip.

The falls were magnificent. However, crossing them meant hard work. Boats, baggage, and supplies all had to be carried up steep paths around the falls.

It was an eighteen-mile hike that took eleven days. Pear cactus thorns bloodied everyone's feet. Rain and hail pounded them. Rattlesnakes lurked in the rocks. The grizzlies were fiercer than ever.

The special iron-frame canoe that Lewis had transported to the Great Falls proved useless.

After a violent wind blew up, most of the skins and hides that lined the iron frame blew off. The canoe was supposed to carry 7,700 pounds of cargo. However, it leaked so much that Lewis sadly wrote: "I . . . ordered her to be sunk in the water . . . and I bid adieu to my boat."

One afternoon, Clark, Charbonneau, and

Sacagawea with Pomp took a walk above the falls. Sacagawea had been deathly sick, and was just now back on her feet.

Suddenly a storm cloud moved in on them. They all ran for shelter in a deep ravine. An overhead rock ledge protected them from hailstones the size of apples. But they were not out of danger. A flash flood roared down the ravine toward them.

Clark helped Charbonneau and Sacagawea, who was still carrying Pomp, climb up the muddy hillside beside the falls. Then he, too, scrambled to safety. They made it just in time.

The floodwaters that swept down the ravine were fifteen feet high. Their belongings were lost, but Clark had saved their lives. Still he worried about his friend, Sacagawea, whom he called Janey. She was cold and soaking wet. But she was young and strong, and she survived.

CHAPTER 7
A Homecoming

Toward the end of July 1805, Sacagawea knew exactly where they were. It was the place where the Minnetaree warrior had captured her. The Corps kept going until they arrived at Montana's Three Forks, where the Missouri River began. By now, the Corps had traveled some two thousand miles on the Missouri River. They were nearing the Rocky Mountains.

For a week they traveled up one of the forks that they'd named the Jefferson River. Then Sacagawea saw a broken-down wickiup in an abandoned Shoshone camp. She knew her Shoshone tribe had been at this very spot. Lewis selected three of the Corps' members, and off they went to find the Shoshones.

Days passed, and they didn't return. Everyone was concerned.

On August 17, 1805, Clark, Charbonneau, and Sacagawea, with Pomp, were walking on the riverbank. Suddenly, two horsemen rode up. One rider was the Corps member who had left with Lewis days ago. The other was an Indian, a Shoshone. Lewis and his men had found the Shoshones!

It was time to get to work. With Lewis and Clark reunited, the men began constructing a camp on the Beaverhead River called Camp Fortunate. It was named for their good fortune in finding the Shoshone people.

Once again, Sacagawea was of great help. Lewis and Clark asked her to translate during their meetings with the Shoshones. Their first meeting was held with everyone seated in a circle under the shade of a pirogue sail. When the Shoshone chief spoke for the first time, Sacagawea gasped.

She knew his voice. The chief was her brother, Cameahwait! She jumped up and threw her arms around him. They both wept with joy.

When Sacagawea had caught her breath, she translated for the Corps members. They traded trinkets, medals, guns, and ammunition with the Shoshones for twenty-nine horses and a mule. The deal was done. Now the Corps would be able to cross the Rocky Mountains. The Corps buried their supplies and sank their canoes in a fork of the Jefferson River. Everything would be there waiting for them when they returned.

On August 30, 1805, Sacagawea bid a sad farewell to her brother and her Shoshone people. Did she want to stay? She probably did, but she never complained about continuing on. She was a wife and mother now. Her life centered around Pompy and Charbonneau. Besides, they were going to the Great Waters—the ocean—which she had always wanted to see.

Cameahwait ordered a Shoshone man, Old Toby, and his four sons to lead the Corps over the Rocky Mountains' rugged Bitterroot Mountains by the Lolo Trail. Their trip coming over the Bitterroots on the Lemhi Pass had been so difficult that knowing they would have guides lifted everyone's spirits.

The Continental Divide

Mapmakers often draw a line to show the Continental Divide running along the crest of the Rocky Mountain ranges. It is called a divide because it divides the eastern from the western United States.

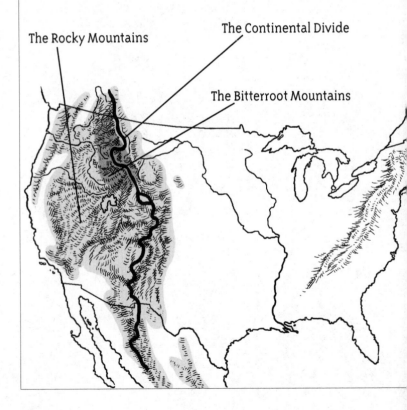

The Rocky Mountains

The Continental Divide

The Bitterroot Mountains

When rain and melted snow raise the rivers on the eastern side of the Continental Divide, the rivers flow east into the Atlantic Ocean and the Gulf of Mexico. The rivers on the western side of the divide also fill up with rain and melted snow, but they flow west into the Pacific Ocean.

There are other subranges within the Bitterroot Range, which itself is part of the Rocky Mountains: the Coeur d'Alène Mountains in the northwest part of the range; the Saint Joe Mountains, the smallest part of the range; the Beaverhead Mountains, which lie east of the Bitterroot Mountains; and the Bitterroot Mountains themselves, which comprise the Northern and Central Bitterroot Ranges.

Any pass over the Continental Divide would be a problem for the Corps. They decided they might as well cross on the Lolo Trail. After a few days' rest, Lewis and Clark and the Corps started out. First it rained, and then it hailed, followed by snow. The water was muddy. At seven thousand feet above sea level, the air was thin. It was hard to breathe, and everyone was hungry. Sharp rocks cut the horses' feet so badly that they couldn't be ridden.

With snow still falling, the Lolo Trail over the Bitterroot pass grew faint. It became harder and harder to follow. Colder weather blew in. Old Toby, the Shoshone guide, got lost and led the Corps three miles out of its way. Horses slipped and fell off the snowy path.

On September 16, the Corps of Discovery woke up to a blizzard. Everyone wrapped rags around their freezing feet. And everyone was hungry.

Clark wrote: "We are continually covered with Snow. I have been wet and as cold in every part as I ever was in my life, indeed I was at one time fearfull my feet would freeze in the thin Mockirsons which I wore."

Cold or not, Clark and six men rode off to hunt. Luckily they met up with generous Walla Walla Native Americans who fed them and gave them meat to take back to the others.

Crossing the Lolo Trail was one of the worst experiences of the journey. But by the end of September, the Bitterroot Range was behind them. They had made it across safely. They were proud of themselves.

Before starting out on the Clearwater River, the men hollowed out five new canoes. They had hundreds of miles still to go.

There were rumors of hostile tribes. However, all they saw were friendly Indians fishing for salmon in the Clearwater River. The sight of Sacagawea with Pomp told the Indians that the white men were peaceable. Clark wrote: "No woman ever accompanies a war party of Indians."

In mid-October, the Corps left the Clearwater River and headed down the Snake River, guided by two Nez Percé chiefs. The chiefs told Lewis and Clark that they would now be traveling by rivers until they reached the Great Waters. The chiefs said that the horses could be left with them. The tribe would care for them until the Corps returned to cross back over the Rocky Mountains. Because Lewis and Clark trusted the Nez Percé, they left all their horses with the tribe.

The Corps continued down the Snake River for a week, fighting boiling rapids, split canoe seams, leaking canoes, and wet baggage. When canoes overturned, gunpowder, papers, food, and clothing were lost. The hungry Corps members lived on dog-meat stew—all but Sacagawea. As a Shoshone, she refused to eat dog meat.

From the Snake River they turned onto the Columbia River. The men cheered. Jefferson had

told Lewis and Clark that the swift currents of the Columbia River would lead them directly to the Pacific Ocean. Still, travel was difficult. The Corps had to fight white-water rapids, waterfalls, narrow channels, and whirlpools. They soon came to a place called Beacon Rock. Though Beacon Rock was more than a hundred miles from the Pacific Ocean, the river water tasted almost as salty as the sea.

Gale winds brought rain and hail for days. A fog blew in. The tides ran higher and higher. Waves crashed over the men. Almost everyone was seasick.

Finally, after fifty-five miles, the river grew easier to navigate. Lewis and Clark halted travel on November 10, 1805, to set up camp. After eleven straight days of rain, the men named their camp Point Distress.

When the skies finally cleared, the Corps pushed off again on the Columbia River. On November 15, the members of the Corps finally saw the Pacific Ocean! Their clothes were in rotted tatters. After weeks of fighting the waves and bailing out the canoes, they were too tired, wet, and numb to celebrate . . . all but Sacagawea. She was thrilled by her first view of the Great Waters.

CHAPTER 8
In and Out of Fort Clatsop

On December 7, 1805, Lewis and Clark had the men start building a fort where they could live for the winter. There was plenty of elk to hunt, and the nearby Clatsop Indians were willing to sell their food. In honor of their neighbors, Lewis and Clark called their new headquarters Fort Clatsop.

It was constructed like all their forts, with logs stacked one above another, with separate huts and rooms as well as a parade ground and a storage area.

The 1805–1806 winter was long, boring, and rainy. Lewis wrote in his journal for hours every day. Clark spent his time drawing maps. The men didn't have much to do except hunt and make clothing and moccasins out of elk hides. That winter they made three hundred pairs of moccasins. Why so many? They had learned the hard way that moccasins only lasted a few days.

Then one day something happened to break the boredom. A dead whale washed up some miles down the beach. Everyone wanted to see the huge creature, including Sacagawea. Lewis and Clark planned to collect whale blubber for eating, and

whale oil for cooking. But the Clatsops claimed the whale was theirs. Lewis and Clark bargained with them. In exchange for the blubber and oil, they gave the Clatsops guns and ammunition.

Another break in the boredom came with the arrival of some Chinooks. Their chief was wearing a magnificent robe made of sea-otter skins. One look at the robe, and both Lewis and Clark wanted it. But the chief demanded blue beads in exchange for the robe. Blue beads were prized by the Indians, who called them "chief beads." However, the explorers had already exchanged all their blue beads for food and horses. They had no blue beads left.

The Chinook chief refused to accept anything but blue beads until he saw the beautiful blue-beaded belt that Sacagawea was wearing. The chief pointed to Sacagawea and made it clear that he would trade his robe for the belt.

Sacagawea treasured her belt. But without saying a word, she unfastened the belt and handed it to the Chinook chief in exchange for his robe. Giving up a prized possession was her way of thanking Lewis and Clark. They had welcomed her on this trip. Clark had saved Pompy, her husband, and herself from drowning back at the Great Falls. Both men had seen her through her last terrible sickness.

The rest of the winter was dreary, wet, and tiring. Of the three months in Fort Clatsop, only twelve days were without rain. The men had reached the end of their journey. Now there was nothing to do but wait out the winter. Then they would begin the trip back east.

President Thomas Jefferson

A replica of the *Discovery*, the keelboat used during the expedition

The Missouri River at Hauser Dam near Helena, Montana

An illustration of the signing of the Louisiana Purchase

Meriwether Lewis

William Clark

A nineteenth-century map of the Lewis and Clark Expedition, prepared using information from William Clark's journals

of small fish which now begin to run and are 93
taken in great quantities in the Columbia R.
about 40 miles above us by means of skiming
or scooping nets. on this page I have drawn
the likeness of them as large as life; it
as perfect as I can make it with my
pen and will serve to give a
general idea of the fish. the
rays of the fins are boney but
not sharp tho' somewhat pointed.
the small fin on the back
next to the tail has no
rays of bone being a   thin mem
bananous pellicle.   the fins next
to the gills have   eleven rays
each. those of the   abdomen have
eight each, those   of the pinnean
are 20 and 2   half formed in front
that of the back   has eleven rays. all
the fins are of   a white colour. the back
is of a bleuish   duskey colour and that of
the the lower   part of the sides and belly
is of a silve=   ry white. no spots on any
part. the   first bone of the gills next
behind the   eye is of a bleuis cast, and the
second of   a light gaald colour nearly white
the puple   of the eye is black and the iris of
a silver   white. the under jaw exceeds the upper
and   the mouth opens to great extent, folding
like   that of the herring. it has no teeth.
the abdomen is obtuse and smooth; in this
differing from the herring, shad anchovy
&c of the Malacapterygious Order & Class
                                            Clupea

A drawing from Lewis's journals

An illustration of Lewis and his men fending off grizzly bears

A Blackfoot tepee

Lewis's and Clark's journals

A sculpture of
Sacagawea and Pompey
at the US Capitol
Visitor Center in
Washington, DC

Pompeys Pillar in Montana

An illustration of Sacagawea guiding the expedition

An American buffalo

A modern replica of Fort Mandan

Inside the replica of Fort Mandan

Prairie dogs

Missouri River's Great Falls

Sioux Indians in Pine Ridge, South Dakota

A nineteenth-century depiction of the Lewis and Clark Expedition

William Clark's grave site in St. Louis, Missouri

A statue of Lewis and Clark in Seaside, Oregon

CHAPTER 9
The Return Trip

On March 23, 1806, the Corps started happily for home. They had been away for almost two years. At least from now on, every mile they traveled brought them closer to the end of their journey.

Earlier, when traveling west, the Columbia River's swift current had cut down their travel time. But now, on the way back east, they had to paddle against the river's swift current. This made travel slow. Melted snow had raised the river ten feet, and it rained every day, raising the river even more.

When the Corps couldn't paddle their canoes through one stretch of rapids, they walked on shore, towing their canoes behind them. From high above, Chinook Indians pelted stones down on them. The Chinooks would also sneak in at night and steal whatever they could from the Corps' supplies. The situation got so bad that Lewis and Clark told the men to shoot any Chinook caught stealing.

At the same time, conditions on the Columbia River grew more difficult. The Corps had to continue on foot. On April 24, 1806, Lewis and Clark ordered the men to hide or sink their canoes. They then traded what things of value they still had. For two cooking pots, the Chinooks gave them ten packhorses.

Upon reuniting with their old friends, the Walla Wallas, the Corps members gained twenty-three more horses. At a party, everyone danced,

even Pomp, who had been walking on his own for some time. He was a cheerful and happy child, and when he did anything for the first time, the men were as proud of him as if he'd been family. Of all the men, Clark was the fondest of the boy. He called him "Little Pomp," or "my little dancing boy."

And then Pomp fell sick with a high fever and a badly swollen sore throat. Fearing he might die,

Sacagawea never left him. Clark, who also stayed by his side, gave Pomp the medicine that Lewis had bought in Philadelphia. It worked! Although his recovery was slow, Pomp got better.

Word spread among the tribes that Captain Clark could heal the sick, and they lined up to be treated. They paid Clark in roots, berries, dogs, and horses, all of which he gratefully accepted.

Late May snow blocked the Rocky Mountains. The Nez Percé chiefs told Lewis and Clark not to travel any farther until the snow melted along the Bitterroot Mountains' Lolo Trail. But Lewis, Clark, and the Corps members didn't want to wait. They left camp on June 15. Thanks to the Nez Percé, each member of the Corps rode a horse and led a packhorse. But the weight of the horses broke through the crust of the snow.

Beneath that crust, the snow was twelve to fifteen feet deep. When Lewis and Clark realized there was no grass for the horses, they had the Corps turn back.

Nine days later, they started out again. Now the crusted snow held their horses' weight. By June 29, they were at the Lolo Trail's warm springs. Hot, bubbling water from the springs drew everyone in to ease sore muscles and tired

backs. What a treat! Smiles broke out on every face, especially Pomp's. But how hard it was to climb out and start traveling in the snow again!

In only six days, their Nez Percé guides had led them 150 miles through deep snow. To regain their strength, for a few days the Corps rested along a branch of the Bitterroot River at a camp in what is now Montana. They had last stopped there in September 1805 on their way to the Pacific Ocean and had named the camp Travellers Rest.

Taking a few days off gave the Corps members a needed break.

On July 3, Lewis and Clark split up the Corps to explore. Lewis led Seaman and nine men on horses north on a route alongside the Missouri River. Clark, Sacagawea and Pomp, Charbonneau, York, and eighteen other men, with forty-nine horses, headed south on horseback for the Yellowstone River.

They were once again in Shoshone country. Sacagawea led Clark's party to a gap in the mountains. She said it was a shortcut to their old Camp Fortunate. On July 8, they arrived at the camp. Months ago, they had sunk their canoes and hidden food, supplies, and tobacco nearby. Everything was still there. While the soldiers repaired their canoes, Sacagawea dug up roots for food. Then, two days later, after gathering up everything, they headed out again.

CHAPTER 10
Setbacks

Clark's party was soon on the Jefferson River. Half of the party rode the horses, and half canoed, keeping each other in sight. On July 13, they all reached the Three Forks of the Missouri. Clark, Sacagawea and Pomp, Charbonneau, York, and eight other men were to ride to the Yellowstone River with the forty-nine horses. The remaining ten men would canoe down the Missouri River to meet Lewis.

The Nez Percé guides rode off for home, leaving Sacagawea as the guide. She pointed out another shortcut, a gap in the mountains. Sacagawea had now safely led Clark and his party more than forty miles.

The next leg of the trip home was the

Yellowstone River. On July 25, they saw a high sandstone bluff that Clark immediately named Pompy's Tower, later changed to Pompeys Pillar. It was about 150 feet high with a base that covered some two acres. Clark carved *W. Clark* and *July 25, 1806* on the bluff. His signature and that date remain there today.

After four days of riding, there was another setback. Crow Indians stole twenty-four of their finest horses. Clark ordered four men to choose the best remaining horses and ride down to Fort Mandan. They were to spread the news that Clark's group was on its way.

From then on, Clark, Sacagawea, Pomp, Charbonneau, and the remaining men traveled down the Yellowstone River in the canoes the men had repaired. Carried eastward by the river's strong current, they made good time.

Lewis was to meet Clark where the Yellowstone River flowed into the Missouri River. When Clark arrived, Lewis wasn't there. But the mosquitoes were, and how they attacked! Clark left Lewis a note before he and his group escaped the mosquitoes and continued down the Missouri River. Clark's note said he would join Lewis at the Great Falls.

A few days later, the four soldiers who had been sent ahead to Fort Mandan met up with Clark, Charbonneau, Sacagawea, and Pomp. The soldiers had traveled down the river hoping they would catch up with Clark. Because Indians had stolen their horses, the men had killed some elk and buffalo and stretched their skins over wooden circular frameworks to make what the Indians called bull boats. When the skins dried, each bull boat could carry a surprising number of people.

While Clark and his group were traveling south down the Missouri River, Lewis and three soldiers headed north in order to pick up the red pirogue. But when they found it, the boat was in such bad condition that it couldn't be used. They left it behind and continued on horseback.

They had been warned that they were in dangerous Blackfoot Indian country. Sure enough, one night, the Blackfeet came and stole seven of their horses. Jefferson had ordered Lewis and Clark not to kill any Indians. But when

the Blackfeet also tried to steal the men's guns, a battle broke out. One of the soldiers stabbed a Blackfoot to death. Lewis shot and killed a second Blackfoot.

Lewis and his three men left Blackfoot country in a hurry. The four men rode one hundred miles at top speed to the Great Falls, pursued most of the way by the Blackfeet. The rest of Lewis's party joined them at the Great Falls. There, they found the white pirogue where they had hidden it the year before.

On August 11, Lewis and his men pushed off down the Missouri River to meet Clark. On the way, Lewis and another man stopped to hunt elk. Going in different directions, the other man— who had poor eyesight—shot what he thought was an elk. Only it wasn't an elk. His bullet had hit Lewis in the rear end!

Although Lewis could hardly walk, he and his men reconnected with Clark. The two groups

had been separated for forty days. Forty days! Although in terrible pain, Lewis was never happier than when he saw the smiling face of William Clark. It was a joyous reunion for the cocaptains.

CHAPTER 11
Arriving Home

Lewis, Clark, and the Corps traveled down the Missouri River together, just as they had started out. On September 23, 1806, they arrived at the camp near St. Louis, where they had spent the winter of 1803–1804 before their journey had begun. Their appearance came as a surprise to the settlers. Most Americans had given up all hope that they were still alive. But they were very much alive and were greeted as heroes. Clark wrote: "We Suffered the party to fire off their pieces [guns] as a Salute to the Town."

Sacagawea was one of the heroes. She had rescued Clark's papers, notes, and scientific samples from the water when their pirogue

overturned. She had translated for Lewis and Clark when they bargained for horses with the Shoshone. She had led the Corps for many miles over land she had known as a child.

Sacagawea knew which plants were poisonous and which were safe. The berries and fruit she picked for the men kept them healthy. Sacagawea had mended the men's breeches and shirts and made them moccasins from animal skins. And Sacagawea, a young mother with a baby, had been a sign to other Indians that the Corps of Discovery came in peace. Maybe the most important of all, she and Pomp had brought a warm feeling of home and family to the soldiers. Just their presence cheered everyone

Later, Clark wrote to Charbonneau that his wife "deserved a greater reward for her attention and services on that route than we had in our power to give her."

When Lewis and Clark finally met with President Jefferson, they told him about almost two hundred plants unknown to American scientists. They described more than 120 animals unknown until then: bison, bighorn sheep, grizzly bears, prairie dogs, mountain goats, coyotes, jackrabbits, porcupines, pronghorn antelope, bull snakes, terns, trumpeter swans, Lewis's woodpeckers, steelhead salmon trout, and more.

What Happened to Sacagawea, Charbonneau, and Pomp?

On its return journey, on August 14, 1806, the Corps reached the Mandan villages. It was time for Sacagawea, Charbonneau, and Pomp to bid good-bye to the men with whom they'd traveled for almost two years. Even though Charbonneau was given $500 and 320 acres of land for serving as an interpreter, Sacagawea was not paid for her valuable role in the expedition. In 1809, Charbonneau moved his family to St. Louis, where Clark also lived. Not long after, Charbonneau and Sacagawea decided to return to the upper Missouri, so Charbonneau sold his land to Clark for $100 and took a job with the Missouri Fur Company. Pomp remained in St. Louis with Clark to receive an education. He later traveled to Europe with a German prince before returning to the frontier.

Charbonneau and Sacagawea were living in what is now South Dakota when Sacagawea died from an illness on December 20, 1812, at the age of twenty-five. This was not long after she had given birth to a daughter, Lisette. Very little is known about Lisette's life, except that both she and Pomp were legally adopted by Clark. Charbonneau lived to be at least eighty years old, but it is unknown where or when he died. Pomp was sixty-one when he died of pneumonia while traveling from California to Montana.

Lewis and Clark had also learned a great deal about the different Western tribes. They repeated Indian words and phrases. They described Indian clothing, ceremonies, and how and where the tribes lived. They reported which tribes got along and which tribes didn't.

It must have been a disappointment to Jefferson that the Corps didn't discover a water route to the

Pacific Ocean. Still, in twenty-eight months, their expedition had traveled a round trip of some eight thousand miles. They had survived in wilderness where no white man had ever been before. What the expedition had accomplished was amazing.

The explorers had gathered all sorts of scientific information. Despite the Indians' presence there, the United States now laid claim to vast Western lands.

As time passed, thousands of American pioneer families traced the expedition's trail west to start a new life. Hoping to get rich, traders,

trappers, hunters, and explorers also headed west following Clark's accurate and detailed maps. Jefferson praised the cocaptains' success: "Never did a similar event excite more joy through the United States."

The Lewis and Clark Expedition changed the face of the American West forever.

Timeline of the Lewis and Clark Expediti[on]

1803	The Louisiana Purchase more than doubles the size of th[e] United States
	President Thomas Jefferson chooses Meriwether Lewis t[o] lead the Journey of Discovery, later known as the Lewis and Clark Expedition
May 1804	The Corps of Discovery departs St. Louis for the West
Aug 1804	Sergeant Charles Floyd dies of a burst appendix
Nov 1804	Fort Mandan is built in what is now North Dakota
Feb 1805	Toussaint Charbonneau and Sacagawea join the Corps
	Sacagawea gives birth to a boy, Jean Baptiste (nicknamed Pomp)
Apr 1805	Several Corps members return to President Jefferson to deliver cargo and report on the expedition's findings
June 1805	Discovery of the Great Falls of the Missouri River
Aug 1805	Lewis and other Corps members get horses from the Shoshone tribe
Sept 1805	The Corps faces challenges crossing the Bitterroot Mountains
Nov 1805	The Corps sees the Pacific Ocean
Dec 1805	Fort Clatsop is built in what is now Oregon
Mar 1806	The men begin traveling east to return home
May 1806	Lewis and Clark halt their journey due to snow blocking the Rocky Mountains
Sept 1806	Lewis, Clark, and the Corps reach St. Louis, where they ar[e] greeted as heroes

Timeline of the World

The United States capital moves from Philadelphia to Washington, DC	1800
John and Abigail Adams move into the White House	
Thomas Jefferson becomes the third president of the United States	1801
The US Military Academy opens at West Point, New York	1802
Beethoven begins writing his third symphony	1804
Vice President Aaron Burr kills Alexander Hamilton in a duel	
Thomas Jefferson is reelected as president	
Napoleon Bonaparte crowns himself Emperor of France	
Napoleon is crowned king of Italy	1805
Noah Webster publishes his first English dictionary	1806
Robert Fulton invents the steamboat	1807
James Madison is elected president of the United States	1808

Bibliography

*Books for young readers

Appleman, Roy E. *Lewis and Clark: Historic Places Associated with Their Transcontinental Exploration (1804–1806)*. Washington, DC: United States Department of the Interior, National Park Service, U.S. Government Printing Office, 1975.

Bakeless, John. *The Journals of Lewis and Clark*. New York: Penguin, 1964.

Bergon, Frank, ed. *The Journals of Lewis and Clark*. New York: Penguin Putnam, 2003.

*Blumberg, Rhoda. *The Incredible Journey of Lewis and Clark*. New York: Scholastic, 1993.

*Bursell, Susan. *The Lewis and Clark Expedition*. Nankato, MN: Capstone Press, 2002.

Duncan, Dayton, and Ken Burns. *Lewis and Clark: The Journey of the Corps of Discovery: An Illustrated History*. New York: Alfred A. Knopf, 1997.

Holloway, David. *Lewis and Clark and the Crossing of North America*. New York: Saturday Review Press, 1974.

Jones, Landon Y., ed. *The Essential Lewis and Clark*. New York: HarperCollins, 2002.

Schmidt, Thomas, and Jeremy Schmidt. *The Saga of Lewis and Clark: Into the Uncharted West: An Illustrated History*. New York: DK Publishing/Tehabi Books, 1999.

Thorp, Daniel B. *Lewis and Clark*. New York: Metro Books/Michael Friedman Publishing Group, 1998.

Turner, Erin H. *It Happened on the Lewis and Clark Expedition*. Guilford, CT: Globe Pequot Press, 2003.

http://www.pbs.org/lewisandclark/inside/saca.html
http://www.pbs.org/lewisandclark/inside/tchar.html
http://www.pbs.org/lewisandclark/inside/jchar.html